INDUSTRIAL
STRENGTH
COLORING BOOK

Gear up to break the coloring mold!

ROBERT PIZZO

Quill
Driver
Books

Fresno, California

Industrial Strength Coloring Book
Copyright ©2016 by Robert Pizzo. All rights reserved.

Published by Quill Driver Books,
an imprint of Linden Publishing

2006 South Mary, Fresno, California 93721
559-233-6633 / 800-345-4447
QuillDriverBooks.com

Quill Driver Books and Colophon
are trademarks of Linden Publishing, Inc.

ISBN 978-1-61035-288-8

Printed in the United States
First Printing
Library of Congress Cataloging-in-Publication Data on file

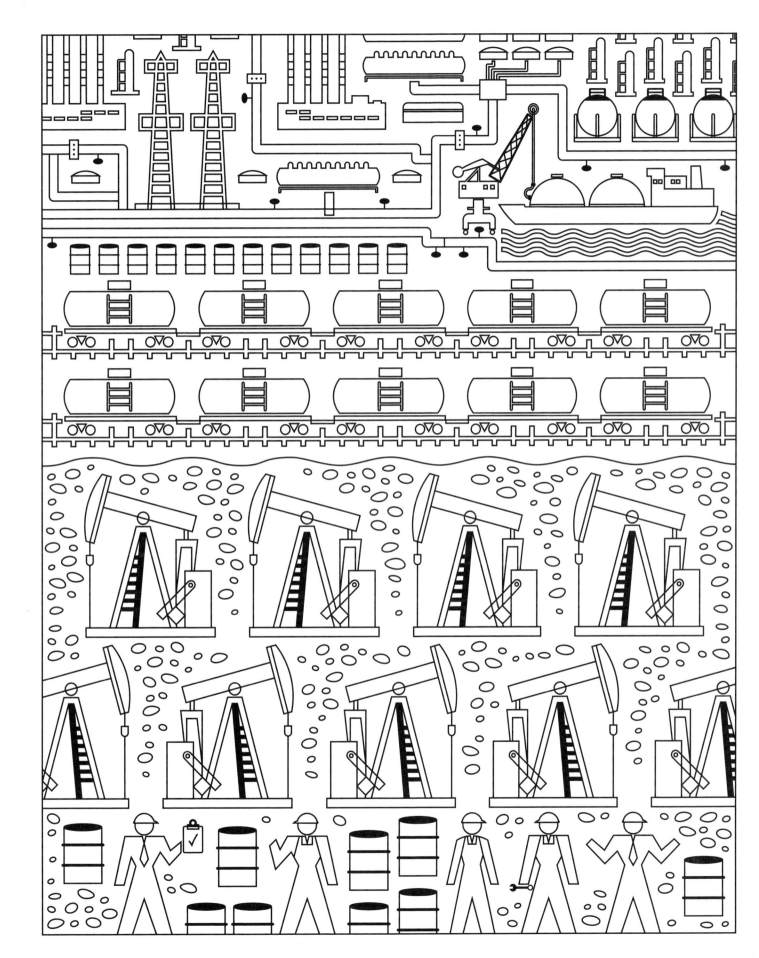

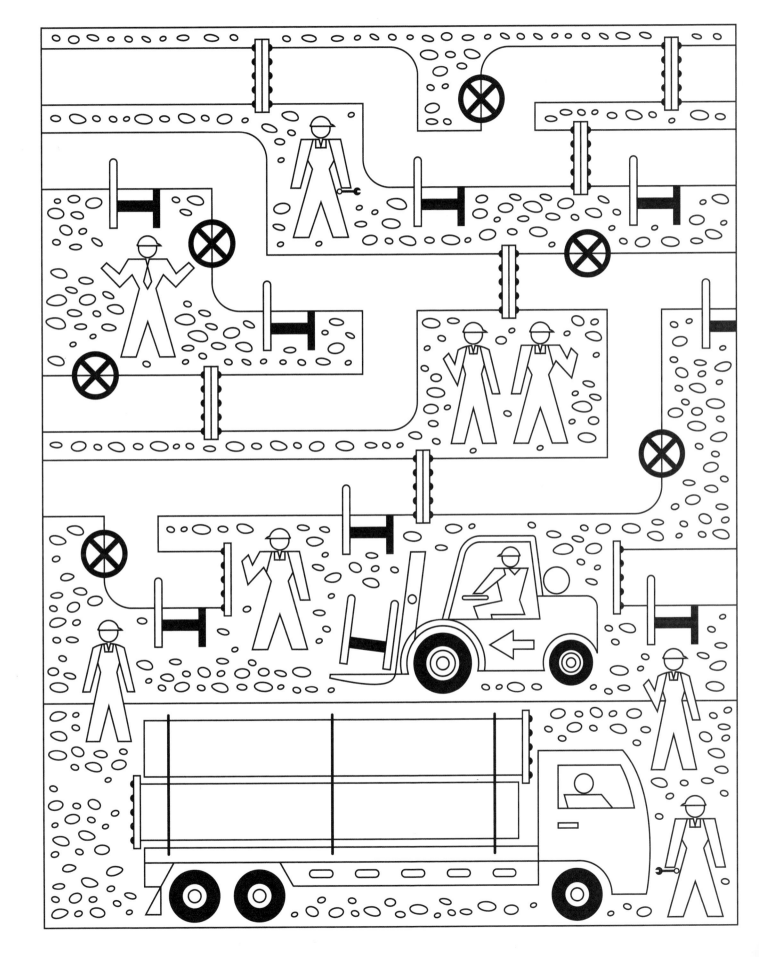

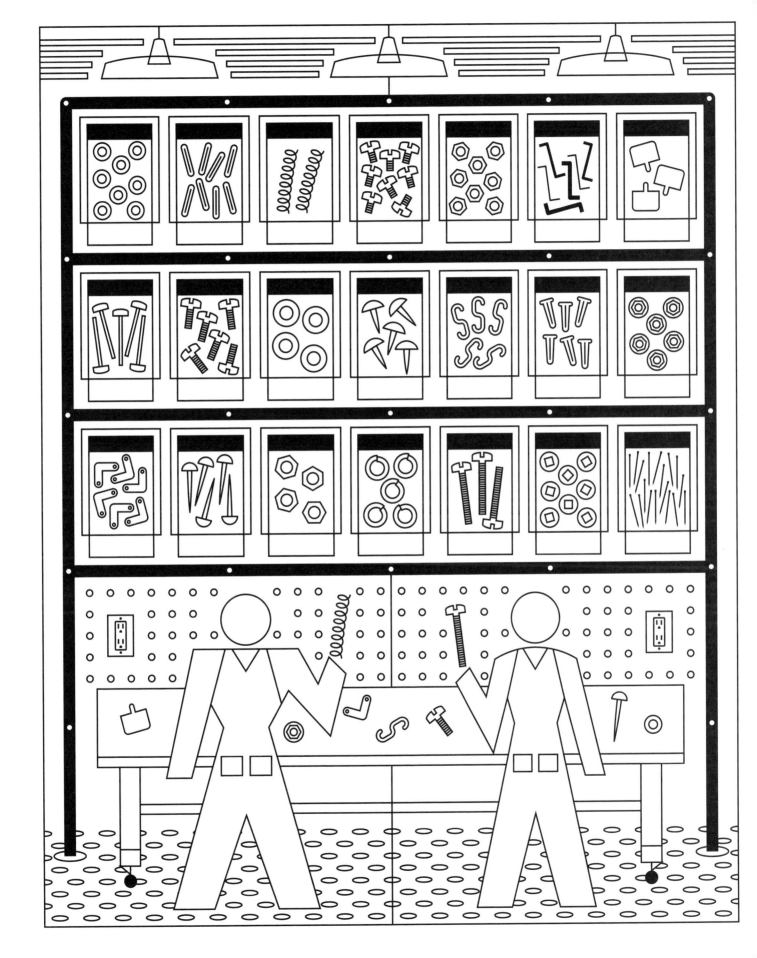

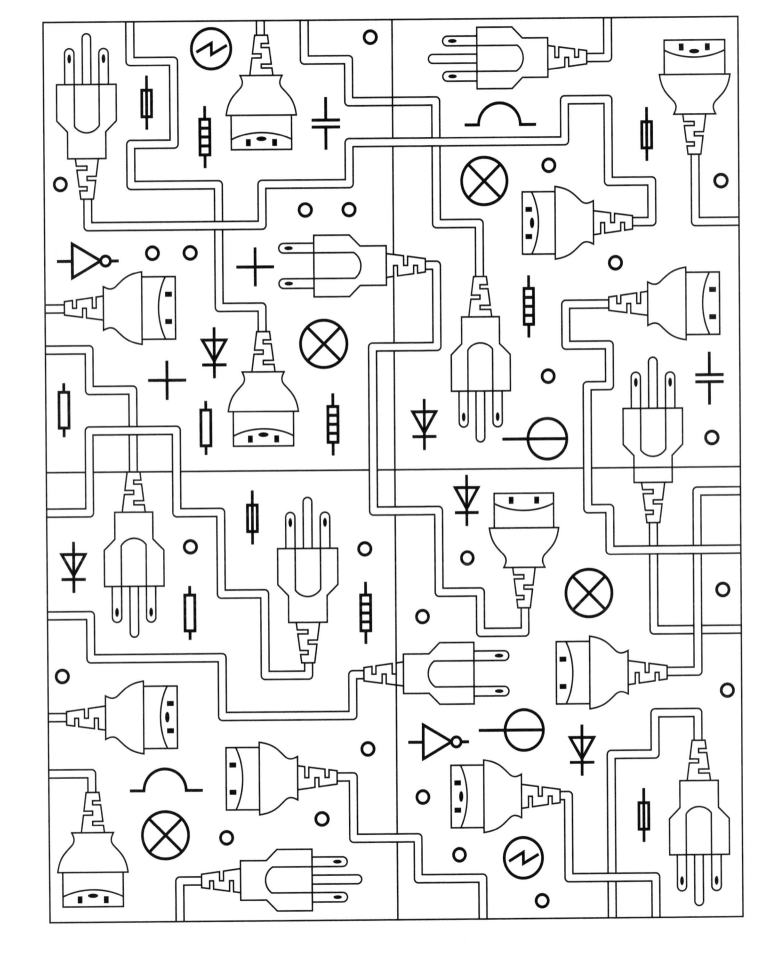

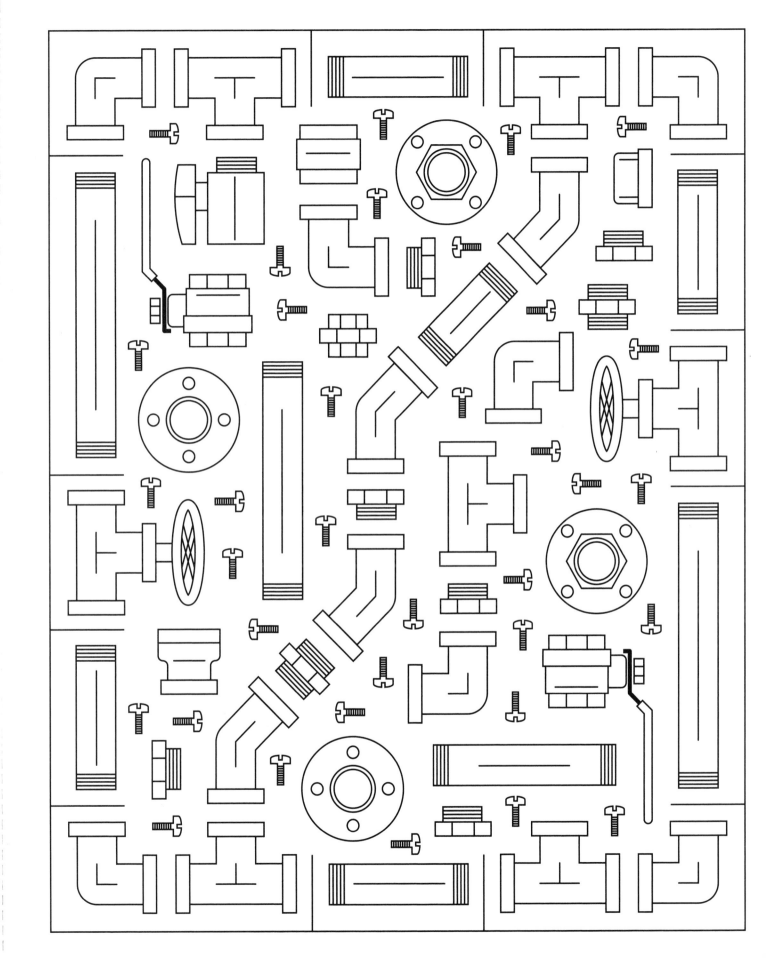

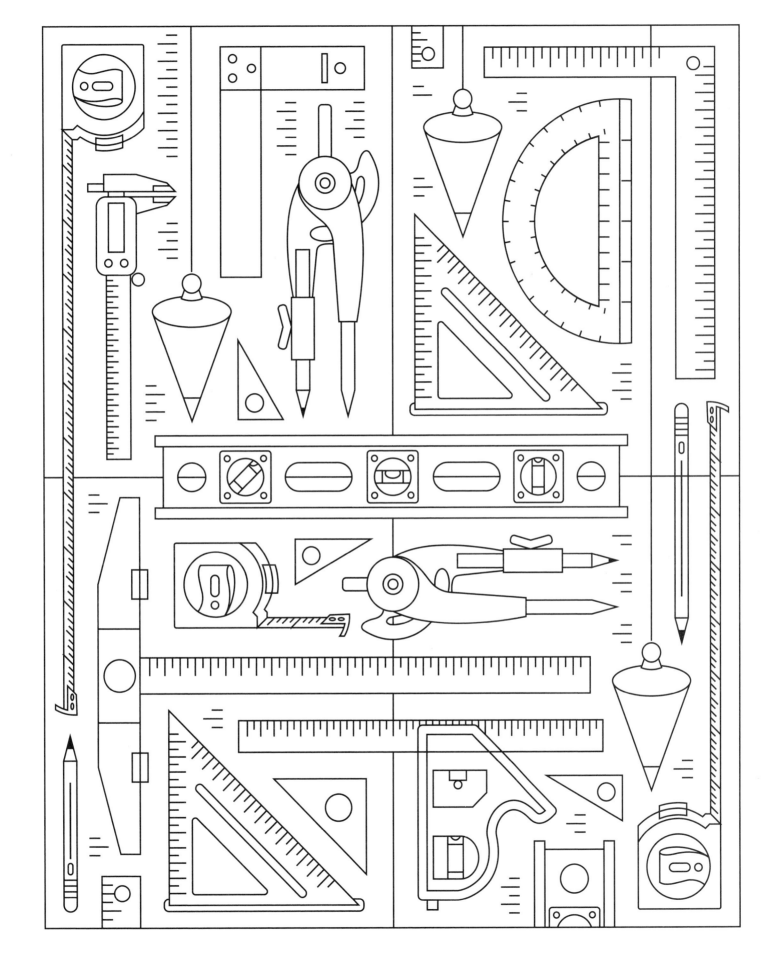

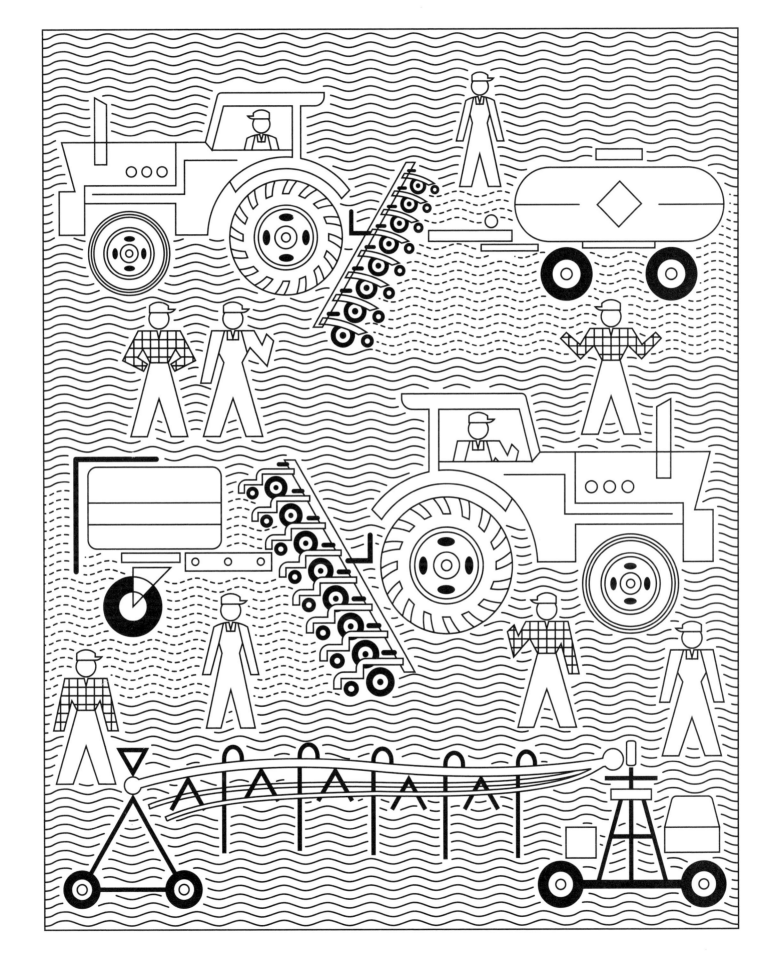

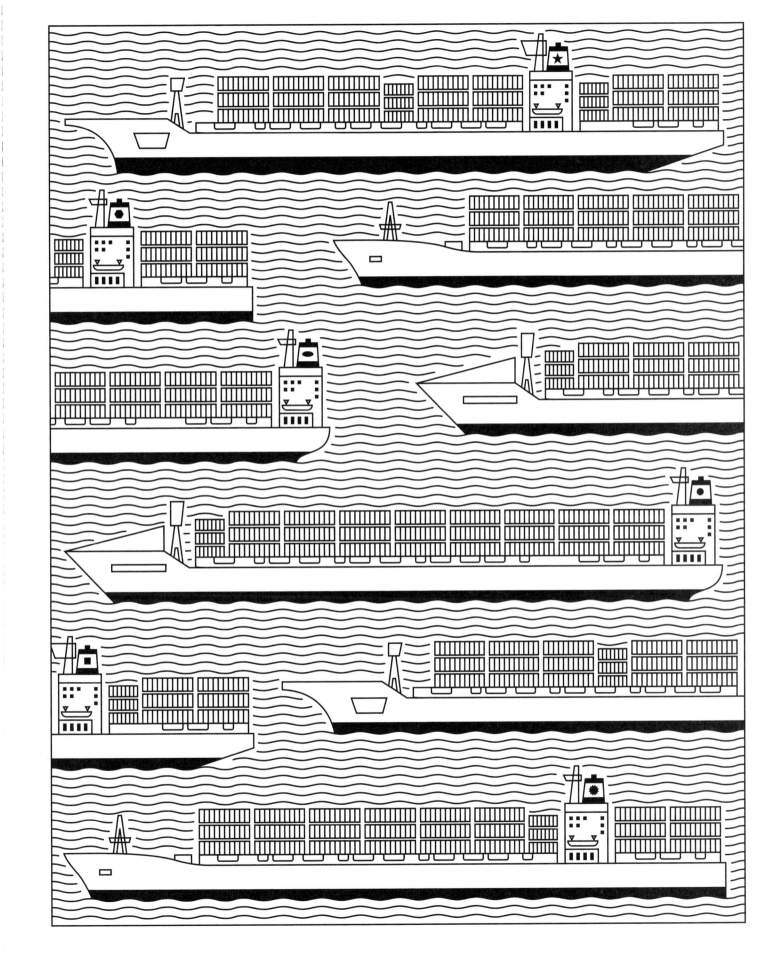

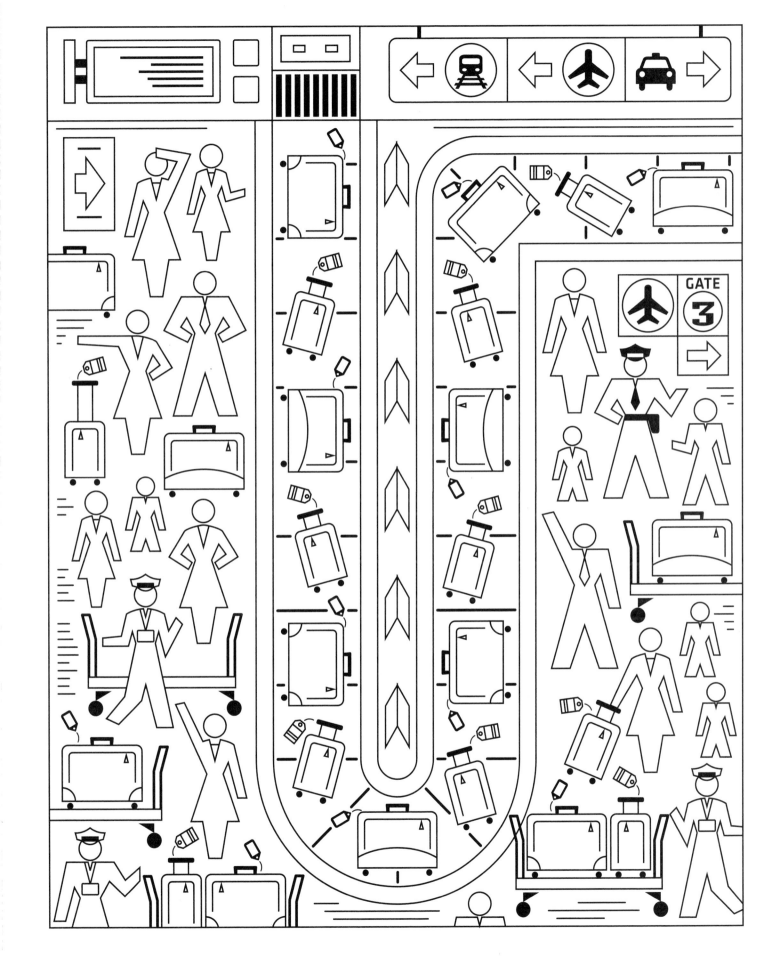

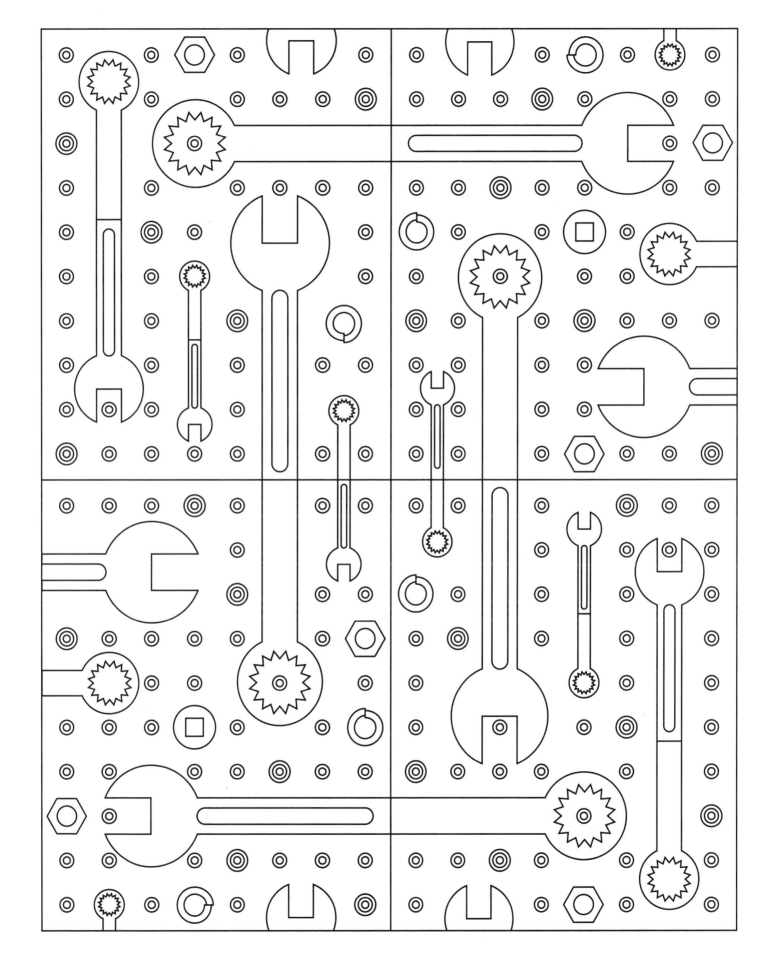

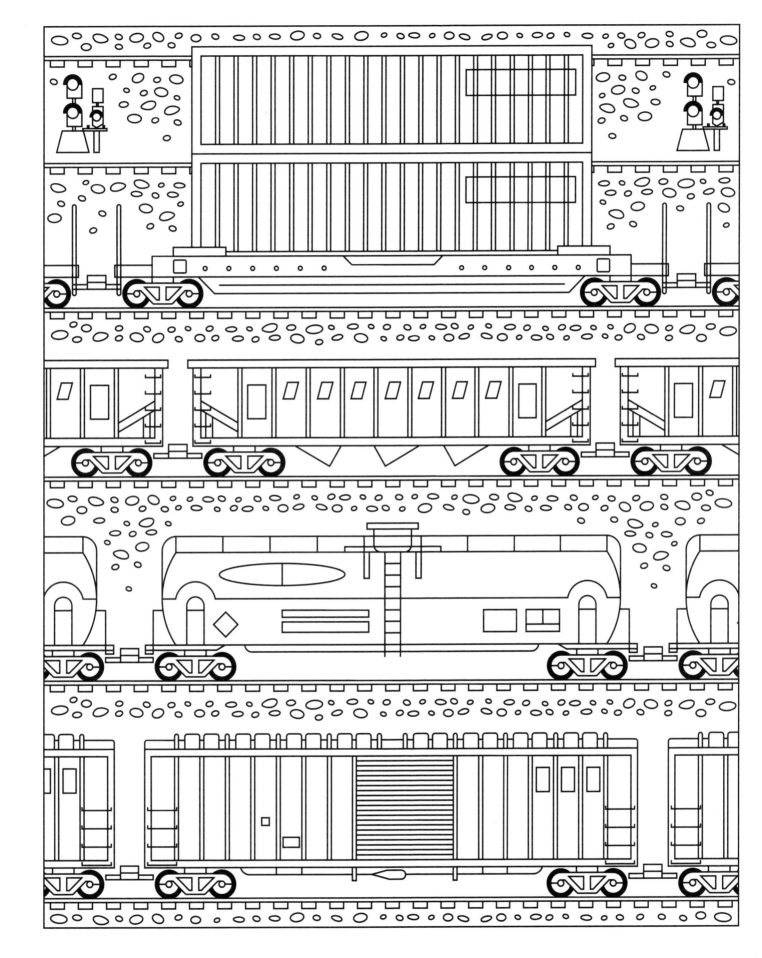

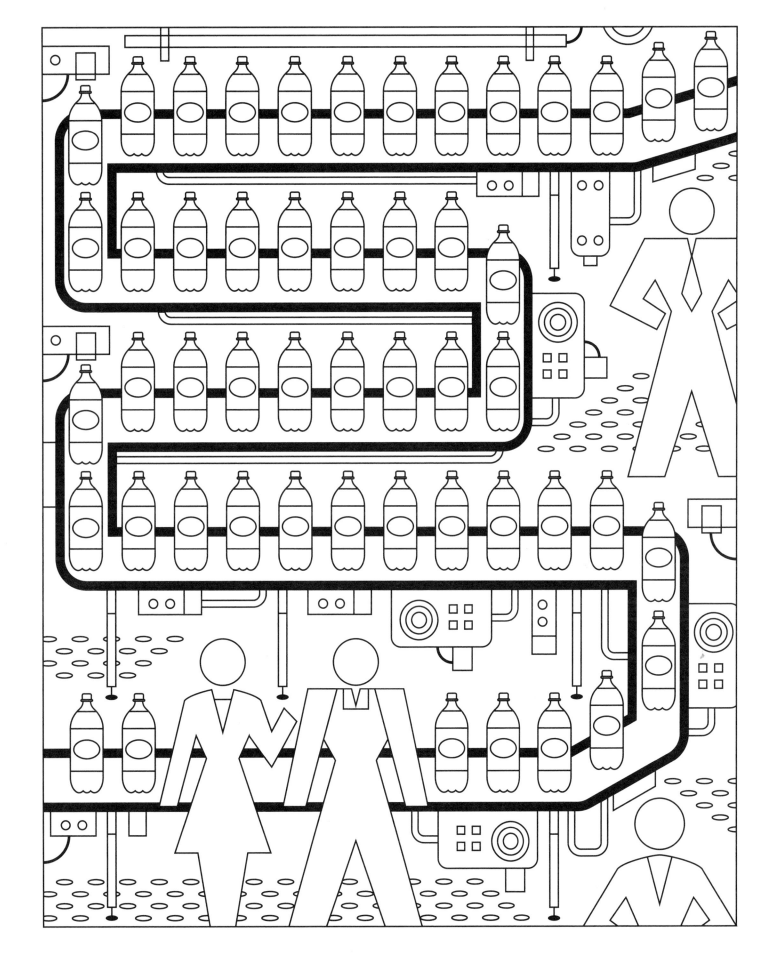

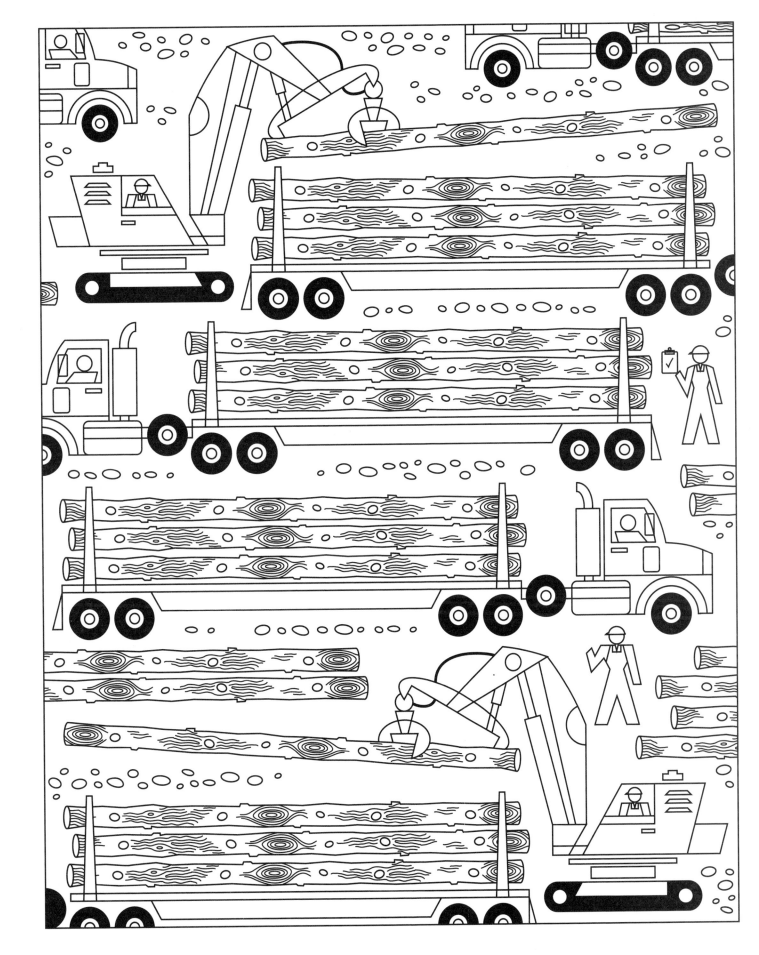

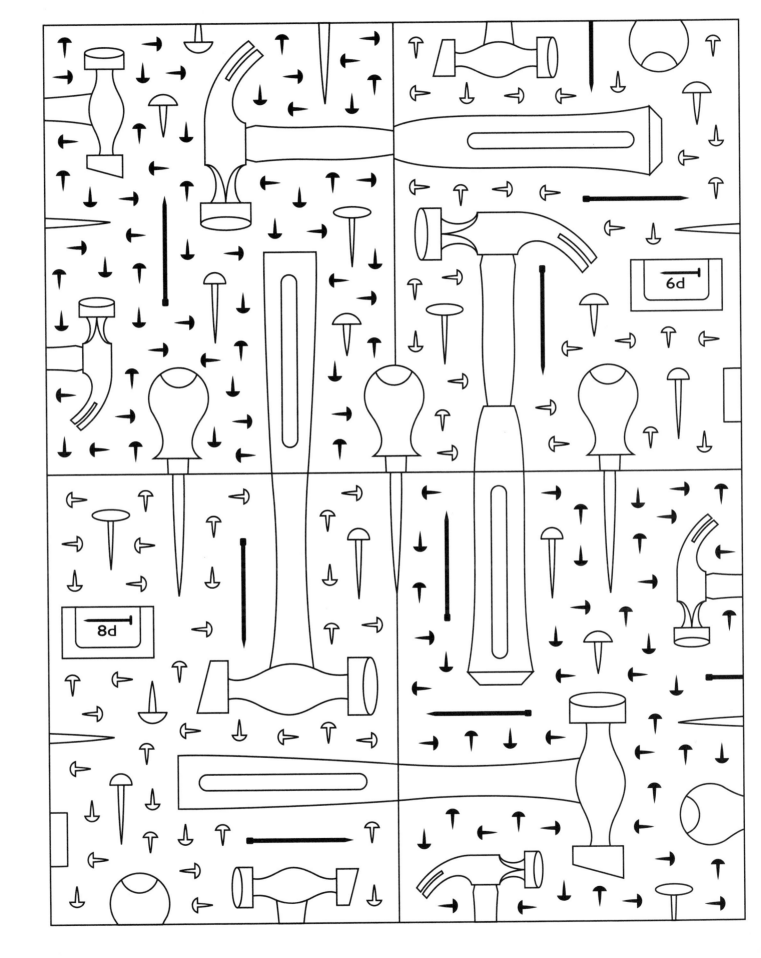

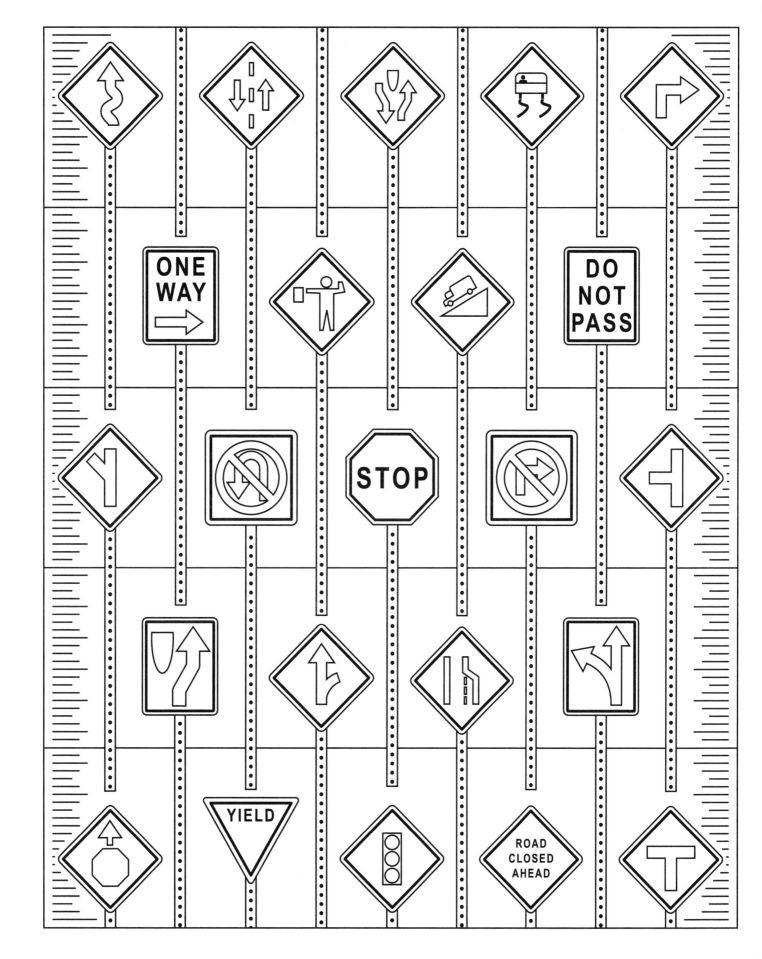

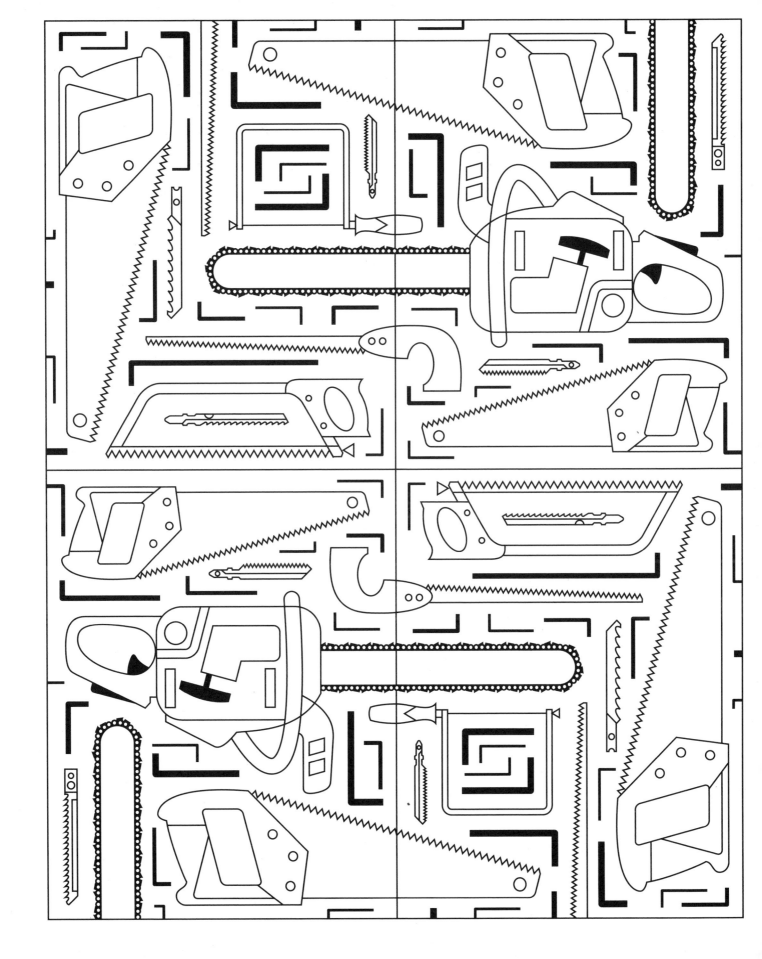

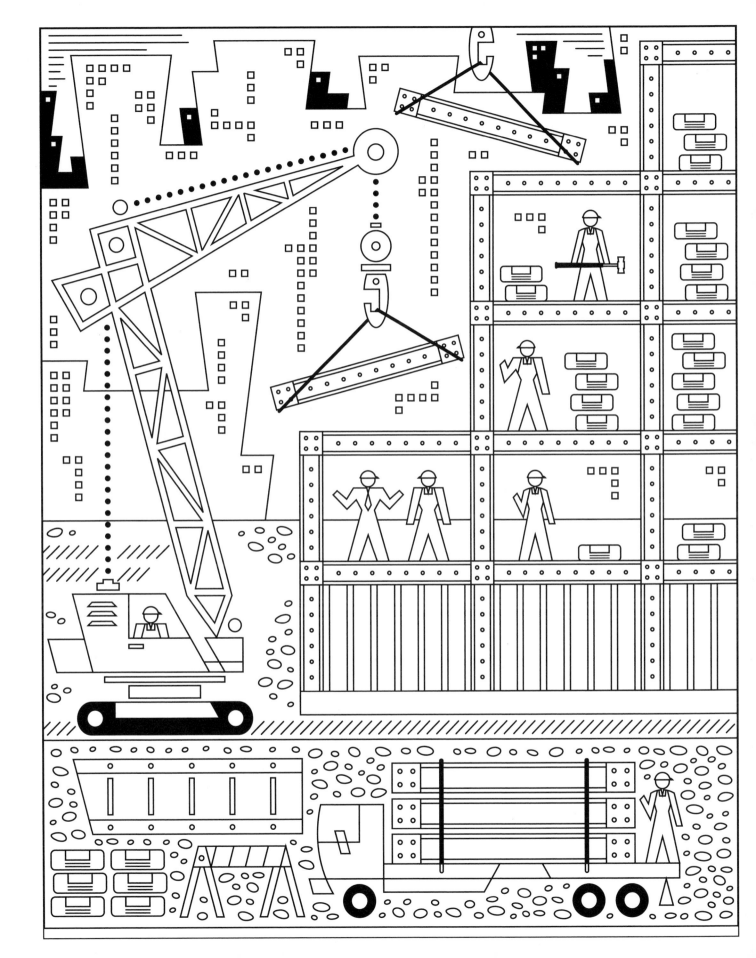

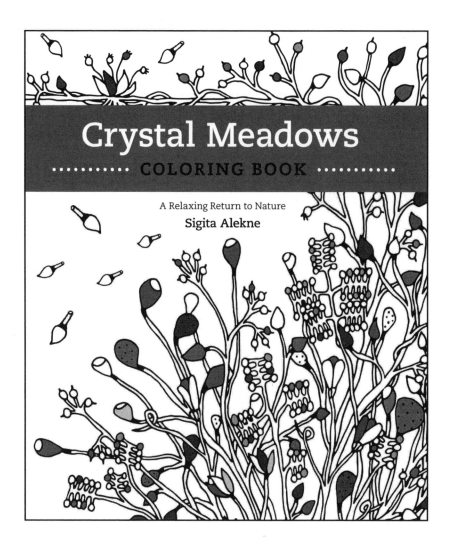

Crystal Meadows
COLORING BOOK

A Relaxing Return to Nature
Sigita Alekne

In a world of constant motion and distraction, we all yearn for a return to the calming world of nature. Take a restorative excursion into the organic world of *Crystal Meadows Coloring Book*. Lose yourself in intricate, otherworldly images of plants, flowers, and trees. Designed by Lithuanian artist Sigita Alekne, the images in *Crystal Meadows Coloring Book* reflect Alekne's unabashed love of nature and living things. Thick, high-quality paper, printed on only one side, gives you a smooth, firm coloring surface with no bleed-through, and perforated pages let your share and preserve your creative work. Like a cool walk into a primeval forest, *Crystal Meadows Coloring Book* will calm your restless spirit and refocus your artistic mind.